COOL CARS

BMW

BY DALTON RAINS

WWW.APEXEDITIONS.COM

Copyright © 2026 by Apex Editions, Mendota Heights, MN 55120. All rights reserved. No part of this book may be reproduced or utilized in any form or by any means without written permission from the publisher.

Apex is distributed by North Star Editions:
sales@northstareditions.com | 888-417-0195

Produced for Apex by Red Line Editorial.

Photographs ©: Pixabay, cover; Shutterstock Images, 1, 4–5, 8–9, 13 (right), 13 (left), 14, 15, 16–17, 18–19, 20–21, 22–23, 24–25, 26, 29; Matthias Schrader/AP Images, 6; Steve Vidler/Mauritius Images GmbH/Alamy, 10–11; iStockphoto, 12

Library of Congress Control Number: 2024952630

ISBN
979-8-89250-518-5 (hardcover)
979-8-89250-554-3 (paperback)
979-8-89250-625-0 (ebook pdf)
979-8-89250-590-1 (hosted ebook)

Printed in the United States of America
Mankato, MN
082025

NOTE TO PARENTS AND EDUCATORS

Apex books are designed to build literacy skills in striving readers. Exciting, high-interest content attracts and holds readers' attention. The text is carefully leveled to allow students to achieve success quickly. Additional features, such as bolded glossary words for difficult terms, help build comprehension.

TABLE OF CONTENTS

CHAPTER 1
A CAR FOR THE FUTURE 4

CHAPTER 2
HISTORY 10

CHAPTER 3
SEDANS 16

CHAPTER 4
OTHER MODELS 22

COMPREHENSION QUESTIONS • 28
GLOSSARY • 30
TO LEARN MORE • 31
ABOUT THE AUTHOR • 31
INDEX • 32

CHAPTER 1

A CAR FOR THE FUTURE

A gleaming gold car pulls out of a garage. It's a BMW Vision Next 100. Even the wheels are covered in gold. But the covering is flexible. It stretches as the wheels turn.

The BMW Vision Next 100 is a concept car. It shows what BMW cars might look like in the future.

Inside, the windshield lights up. It shows information to the driver. It points out cars, people, and objects blocking the road.

MORE WARNINGS

Many triangles cover the Vision's **dashboard**. They flap between white and red. A biker may be on the right. Then triangles on the right will turn red. They'll point to the biker.

The Vision Next 100 was built to celebrate 100 years since the founding of BMW.

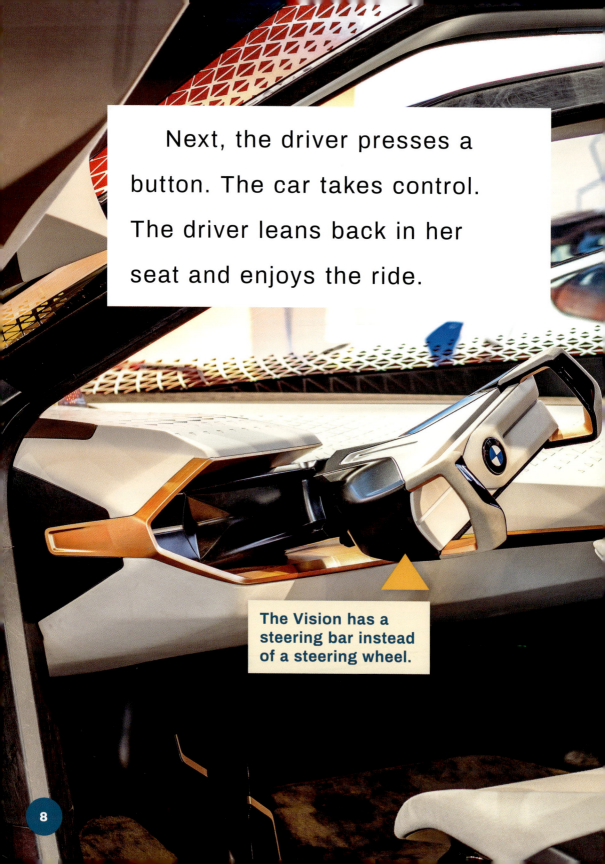

Next, the driver presses a button. The car takes control. The driver leans back in her seat and enjoys the ride.

The Vision has a steering bar instead of a steering wheel.

CHAPTER 2

History

BMW formed in the early 1900s. The company built aircraft engines at first. In the early 1930s, BMW released its first car.

BMW's first car was the 303.

In the 1950s, BMW began selling the Isetta. This tiny car had a bubble shape, and its door opened from the front.

BMW stopped making cars during World War II (1939–1945). Afterward, the company focused on **luxury** cars. BMWs were comfortable and stylish. But they were also fast.

IN THE NAME

BMW started in Bavaria, Germany. Its name stands for "Bavarian Motor Works." The company's headquarters remain in Bavaria today.

BMW's logo borrows the colors and pattern from the Bavarian flag.

BMW released many cars. The 1500 came out in 1961. It combined a sports car with a family **sedan**. BMW made M1s only from 1978 to 1981. But the **supercar** became famous.

Sales of the 1500 saved BMW from going out of business.

The M1 blended German and Italian styles.

FAST FACT

The M2 was sold from 2015 to 2021. It's one of BMW's most well-known modern models.

15

CHAPTER 3

SEDANS

BMW is one of the best-selling luxury car **brands** in the world. The expensive cars are **symbols** of success. The company is famous for its sedans.

In 2023, BMW sold more than 2 million vehicles.

BMW 3 Series sedans are very popular. These cars have sleek bodies. Smooth steering makes driving easy and fun.

BMW has several 3 Series models that people can choose from.

SLEEK SEDANS

Air flows smoothly over a BMW's rounded edges. That makes the cars easier to control. It also helps them drive fast. The cars save energy, too.

Drivers can show off speed with their BMWs. The BMW M8 can put all its power into its rear wheels. This gives the car an extra boost of speed.

The M8 has a top speed of 189 miles per hour (304 km/h).

FAST FACT

The M8 can shoot to 60 miles per hour (97 km/h) in just three seconds.

CHAPTER 4

Other Models

For drivers who like smaller cars, BMW sells several coupe models. They back up the sporty look with powerful engines.

Coupes are smaller than sedans. They are usually considered the sportier option.

The X5 SUV was a top-selling BMW model in 2023.

BMW also sells SUVs. These vehicles have lots of room inside. The BMW X5 is packed with technology, too. It has a hands-free driving option. And it has an internet hotspot.

FAST FACT
Many BMWs have heated seats and steering wheels. Some even have massage chairs.

Several BMWs have **hybrid** engines. Others are all electric. The i3 and iX3 are two examples. BMW is always improving. That's what keeps it among the top luxury car brands.

FAST FACTORIES
BMW has some of the most-advanced factories in the world. Robots help build thousands of cars each day. Many parts are built or put together **automatically**.

◀ In the early 2020s, BMW worked on increasing its sales of electric cars.

COMPREHENSION QUESTIONS

Write your answers on a separate piece of paper.

1. Write a few sentences explaining the main ideas of Chapter 3.

2. Which BMW model would you most like to have? Why?

3. When did BMW release its first car?
    - A. the early 1900s
    - B. the early 1930s
    - C. the early 1960s

4. Why might BMWs be viewed as symbols of success?
    - A. because they are hard to drive
    - B. because they are cheap and common
    - C. because they cost a lot of money

5. What does **flexible** mean in this book?

But the covering is flexible. It stretches as the wheels turn.

- **A.** able to hold very still
- **B.** not able to move easily
- **C.** able to bend without breaking

6. What does **technology** mean in this book?

The BMW X5 is packed with technology, too. It has a hands-free driving option. And it has an internet hotspot.

- **A.** small seats
- **B.** helpful machines
- **C.** big problems

Answer key on page 32.

GLOSSARY

automatically
Done by a machine without being controlled by people.

brands
Companies that are known for making products or services.

dashboard
The part of a car in front of the driver.

hybrid
Machines that can use two different sources of energy, such as gas and electricity.

luxury
Having to do with things that are high quality, comfortable, and often expensive.

sedan
A car that seats at least four people comfortably.

supercar
A car fast enough for racing that can also go on the street.

symbols
Objects or ideas that stand for and remind people of something else.

BOOKS

Morey, Allan. *Inventing Cars*. Focus Readers, 2022.

Peterson, Megan Cooley. *BMW i8*. Black Rabbit Books, 2021.

Webster, Christine. *BMW*. AV2, 2022.

ONLINE RESOURCES

Visit **www.apexeditions.com** to find links and resources related to this title.

ABOUT THE AUTHOR

Dalton Rains is a writer and editor from St. Paul, Minnesota.

INDEX

#
1500, 14
3 Series, 18

B
Bavaria, Germany, 13

C
coupes, 22

I
i3, 27
iX3, 27

M
M1, 14
M2, 15
M8, 20–21

S
sedans, 14, 16, 18–19
supercars, 14
SUVs, 25

V
Vision Next 100, 4, 7–9

W
World War II, 12

X
X5, 25

ANSWER KEY:
1. Answers will vary; 2. Answers will vary; 3. B; 4. C; 5. C; 6. B

32